THE MAMMALS

PREHISTORIC
NORTH AMERICA
THE MAMMALS

HUGH WESTRUP
ILLUSTRATED BY TED FINGER

THE MILLBROOK PRESS ■ BROOKFIELD, CONNECTICUT

Library of Congress Cataloging-in-Publication Data
Westrup, Hugh.
The mammals / by Hugh Westrup ; illustrated by Ted Finger.
p.   cm. — (Prehistoric North America)
Includes bibliographical references and index.
Summary: The story of prehistoric mammals,
where they came from, what the different kinds
were like, and theories about their disappearance.
ISBN 1-56294-546-7
1. Mammals, Fossil — North America — Juvenile literature.
[1. Mammals, Fossil.]   I. Title.   II. Series.
QE881.W475   1995   569'.097 — dc20   95-1960   CIP   AC

Published by The Millbrook Press, Inc.
2 Old New Milford Road, Brookfield, Connecticut 06804

250 MILLION YEARS AGO
the Triassic Period began. The animals of this period were primitive two-legged meat eaters.

208 MILLION YEARS AGO
the Jurassic Period (the Age of Dinosaurs) began. Sauropods—gigantic animals with long necks and small heads—were plant eaters who walked on four legs.

145 MILLION YEARS AGO
the Cretaceous Period began. Plant-eating armored and horned dinosaurs fought for survival with meat-eating giants.

65 MILLION YEARS AGO
the dinosaurs were gone. The Age of Mammals began. Early placentals evolved into the ancestors of the modern horse.

37 MILLION YEARS AGO
the creodonts (early meat-eating mammals) began to give way to the carnivores, such as the tree-climbing dawn dog, whose descendents include wolves, coyotes, and modern dogs.

2 MILLION YEARS AGO
during the Ice Age, huge, hearty animals such as wooly mammoths lived in large numbers near the glaciers of what is now Canada and the northern United States.

12,000 YEARS AGO
human beings followed herds of animals across the Bering Land Bridge into North America.

The author gratefully acknowledges the help and advice of the following people: Stephen Fraser; Professor Christine Janis, University of Chicago; Professor Donald Prothero, Occidental College; Professor Larry Martin, University of Kansas; Dr. Dick Harrington, Canadian Museum of Nature.

THE MAMMALS

A *SMILODON* READY TO POUNCE ON A YOUNG CAMEL.

Holding its body close to the ground, the big saber-toothed cat sneaks through the tall grass. The cat's eyes are fixed on a young camel that has strayed from its herd. Closer and closer to the camel the cat creeps.

Then, in a burst of strength, the big cat leaps into the air and pounces on its prey, knocking the animal to the ground. Grasping the camel with its claws, the cat rears its head and opens wide its powerful jaws. Two long fangs flash in the sunlight.

Bringing its head down, the cat pierces the camel's throat with its fangs. The cat slashes again and again until the camel goes limp. The slower-moving camel is no match for a strong, fierce — and very hungry — predator.

This terrible struggle did not happen on the plains of Africa. It happened here in North America. Before the arrival of human beings, North America was a place you might not recognize. The landscape was different. The climate was different. And so was the wildlife.

For millions of years, North America was home to a grand menagerie of prehistoric mammals as remarkable in their way as the dinosaurs: beavers the size of bears, camels as tall as giraffes, armadillos as big as cars. Scientists refer to the era in which these animals were the world's most powerful occupants as the Age of Mammals.

The Age of Mammals began in North America (and elsewhere) about 65 million years ago. Mammals had been living on Earth for 150 million years by then, but mostly at nature's fringes. The early mammals were small. They made their homes underground or in trees, daring to come out only at night. They *had* to live that way to avoid getting stepped on or eaten by the planet's giant rulers, the dinosaurs.

That all changed, though, when the dinosaurs died out, or became extinct. No longer were the mammals forced to inhabit North America's nooks and crannies. The continent was theirs to explore and inhabit until the Ice Age ended 12,000 years ago.

WINDOWS INTO THE PAST

ow do we know what prehistoric mammals were like? They left us no photographs or videos of themselves. Yet scientists have composed vivid descriptions of prehistoric mammals. Those descriptions were made with the help of preserved teeth and bones.

Most animals decay completely when they die. In some cases, though, a dead animal is washed into a lake, a river, or a sea and covered with sediment—

the mud that settles on the bottom. Or it is covered by wind-blown sand during a storm. The covering of sand or sediment stops the animal's bones from decaying. Instead, water that contains dissolved minerals seeps into tiny holes in the bones. Slowly, the water dissolves the bone material, leaving the minerals in its place. The result is a fossil, a permanent stone copy of the original bone.

Scientists who examine fossil bones are called paleontologists. They spend long hours carefully chiseling fossils out of the ground in which the bones were buried thousands or millions of years ago. Often, a paleontologist will find only a few fossil bones or pieces of a single fossil bone from one animal. Sometimes an entire fossil skeleton will be uncovered.

By comparing fossils with the bones of animals that are alive today, scientists can learn a lot about the looks and behavior of extinct animals. For example, an extinct mammal may have had limbs just like a cheetah's. That would suggest that the extinct mammal was a very fast runner. Or the extinct mammal may have had horselike teeth, suggesting that it grazed on grass.

Fossils also tell scientists about evolution, the process by which animals and plants gradually change over long periods of time. By examining fossils that were created at different periods in history, scientists can tell how animals evolved from one form to another. Two different animals that lived millions of years apart may have had a few similar bones or teeth, suggesting that the two animals were related.

Sometimes, fossils tell us that animals evolved in remarkable directions. Forty-five million years ago, a wolflike mammal named *Harpagolestes* lived in North America. It had a massive head and jaws with unusually long teeth for cutting flesh. *Harpagolestes* belongs to a group of animals that moved from land to water. As the group adapted to life under water, it changed in many ways. It swapped limbs for flippers, for example. However, it kept the long teeth of its earlier relatives. The descendents of *Harpagolestes* were the world's first whales!

Not all fossils are preserved teeth and bones. Some are preserved footprints or burrows. Perhaps the most unusual fossils in North America are found around Harrison, Nebraska. Called devil's corkscrews, they are 9-foot-deep (3-meter) tunnels that spiral downward through the ground. Made 22 million years ago, the tunnels became preserved when their walls turned into a hard, glassy substance that has withstood the destructive power of water and wind.

The ranchers who discovered the weird tunnels had no idea what they were. Then someone found fossil bones of an extinct mammal—a prehistoric beaver—at the bottom of one tunnel. That led scientists to suspect that the spiral tunnels were the bea-

A DEVIL'S CORKSCREW,
OCCUPIED BY A PREHISTORIC
BEAVER FAMILY.

vers' burrows. Teeth marks on the tunnel walls confirmed that suspicion. Apparently, the beavers made the spiral burrows by screwing themselves down into the ground, using their superlong front teeth to scrape away the dirt. At the bottom of each burrow, the beavers carved out chambers and side passages that made the burrow a safe, comfortable home for themselves and their cubs.

■ ■ ■

As you can see, fossils tell us much more than what animals looked like. Each fossil is like a single piece in a giant puzzle. By carefully examining all of these pieces, scientists create a picture of when, where, and how animals lived, what the weather and geography were like, and the kinds of plants that grew. In short, fossils create a window into a world that existed long, long ago.

IN THE BEGINNING

If you could travel backward in time to North America as it was 65 million years ago, you might think you had landed in a kind of paradise. The weather was warm all year round. Flowers bloomed everywhere. Dense tropical forests covered much of the continent.

Most of the mammals that scurried through the forests of this earthly paradise were no bigger than squirrels. Although these early mammals of North America were small, they already bore the basic traits that most mammals have today. Their skin was covered with fur. Their ears had three small bones that gave them excellent hearing. Their skulls had an opening behind each eye socket. The females gave birth to live babies and nursed their young with milk from special mammary glands.

North America's first mammals fell into three groups:

• *Multituberculates.* "Multis" were rodentlike creatures that had large sharp incisors (front teeth) for gnawing on hard plant tissue and complex molars (back teeth) for grinding up the plant material. Newborn multis probably licked milk from the skin around the openings of their mothers' milk glands.

• *Marsupials.* Female marsupials give birth to blind, deaf, and hairless babies that look like pink grubs. The tiny newborns crawl up the outside of the mother's stomach and down into her special pouch (marsupium). There they stay for weeks or months, sucking milk from the mother's nipples and growing to a mature size.

• *Placentals.* Placental mammals are named after a structure, called the placenta, that develops within the mother's body when she is pregnant. Through the placenta, the mother nourishes her unborn young with food and oxygen. At birth, placental babies are more mature than marsupial babies and don't need the protection of a pouch.

PTILODUS (A MULTITUBERCULATE), *PERADECTES* (A MARSUPIAL), AND CHRIACUS (A PLACENTAL) IN A WYOMING FOREST, 60 MILLION YEARS AGO.

Almost all of the ancient mammals described in this book were placentals. Multituberculates decreased in number and eventually became extinct 35 million years ago. Marsupial mammals disappeared from the Northern Hemisphere at about the same time and lived mostly in South America and Australia after that.

PLACENTALS COME OUT OF HIDING ▪ North America's early placental mammals were similar to one another in looks and behavior. Their diet was a mixture of insects, fruit, berries, and shoots.

When the dinosaurs died out, it became much easier for placentals to survive. Their numbers grew, and they evolved in a variety of ways. Many grew bigger. Some began to forage for food in the daytime. Others moved down from trees to the ground.

Some of the early placentals of the Age of Mammals were recognizable ancestors of animals we know today. Among the mammals that stayed in the trees, *Notharctus* stood out. It resembled the lemurs that live in Madagascar today.

You might call *Notharctus* one of your earliest relatives. It was one of the first primates — the group of animals whose family tree includes monkeys, apes, and human beings.

One North American ground-dweller was called *Hyrachyus*. Graceful and slender and a swift runner, *Hyrachyus* was the size of a modern wolf. It was the world's first rhinoceros.

HYRACOTHERIUM, THE FIRST HORSE.

Another ground-dwelling creature was the size of a big house cat. Called *Hyracotherium*, it had a slim head and trunk, short legs, and feet with pads like a dog's. *Hyracotherium* was the start of one of the most successful lines of mammals in North America: the horse.

Notharctus, Hyrochyus, and *Hyracotherium* were just three of many new species that emerged in North America as mammals made the most of what the continent had to offer. In only a short time, the Age of Mammals was well under way.

One hundred and twenty years ago, the fossil bones of an unknown prehistoric creature were dug up in the Uinta Basin of Utah. Big and bulky like a rhinoceros, the creature had blunt, bony knobs on its head and two long fangs sticking out of its mouth.

UINTATHERIUM, AN ADULT AND BABY.

So bizarre was the creature that the people who found it thought they had unearthed a new species of dinosaur. But they hadn't. The creature, named *Uintatherium*, was later identified as an extinct mammal that lived 45 million years ago. Someone once called it "the most grotesque mammal that ever lived."

Poor *Uintatherium*. Though big and ugly, it was simply following a general trend in evolution called Cope's Law. Edward Drinker Cope was a nineteenth-century paleontologist who observed that animals tend to evolve larger body sizes in the course of time. Animals benefit from being larger. Big animals tend to have fewer enemies and an easier time getting around. Their large bodies also burn less energy, so they spend less time hunting for food.

Many mammals became bigger during the Age of Mammals. They also went through other major changes that separated them into a number of distinct groups during the course of 65 million years.

RODENTS ▪ Not all mammals became bigger after the dinosaurs disappeared. Being small has its advantages, too. Small animals can hide in corners and crevices. They can also produce many more babies in a short period of time than large animals can.

Among those mammals that stayed small were the rodents, like squirrels, beavers, rats, and mice. Rodents are known for their large, chisel-like incisors well-suited for gnawing on nuts, seeds, and wood. Rodent teeth never stop growing. As a result, rodents must bite all the time to keep their incisors worn down. If a rodent stops gnawing, its incisors grow so long that it can't close its mouth, and it starves.

The earliest known North American rodents appeared in what is now Wyoming 55 million years ago. They nudged the multituberculates toward extinction and became the most abundant mammals in North America and on the rest of the planet.

UNGULATES ▪ A second group to appear during the Age of Mammals were the ungulates. These were animals with hard growths, or hooves, on their feet.

Uintatherium was an ungulate. So were a large number of long-tailed and piglike animals—the oreodonts—that roamed the woodlands and grasslands of North America for 30 million years. The oreodonts were herbivores (plant eaters), as are all other hoofed animals. Thousands of oreodont fossils have been found in the Badlands of South Dakota.

Some ungulates grew amazing headgear. One ancient bruiser—*Brontops*—had a huge set of horns on its snout. A male *Brontops* probably used his horns to protect himself against predators or to attract females.

Another group of ungulates with elaborate horns (protoceratids) roamed the southern regions of North America. One species, *Syndyoceras*, sported two curved horns on the back of its head and a V-shaped pair on its snout.

A close relative of *Syndyoceras*, called *Synthetoceras*, had a Y-shaped nasal horn that would have made a good slingshot. The males probably used their horns in sparring matches with one another. The winner would become the dominant member of the herd.

Another large group of hoofed animals were the camels. When you hear the word camel, you probably think of the Sahara Desert in Africa. Believe it or not, though, camels got their start here in North America. Forty million years ago, the world's first camel, no bigger than a rabbit, emerged in North America.

In the course of time, some camels grew taller and taller, reaching their peak with *Aepycamelus*, or the "high camel." Able to stretch its neck to a height of 18 feet (5 meters), *Aepycamelus* used its soaring height to eat leaves from the tops of trees, just as giraffes do today.

Many camels migrated from North America to Asia about 2 million years ago. They did so by way of the Bering Land Bridge, a stretch of land that used to connect what are now Alaska and Siberia. But camels continued to live in North America until about 12,000 years ago. Then they vanished mysteriously forever.

OREODONTS GRAZING IN A FIELD, IN THE COMPANY OF *MESOHIPPUS*, ANOTHER EARLY HORSE (FAR LEFT).

CREODONTS AND CARNIVORES ▪ Many prehistoric mammals were plant eaters. Other prehistoric mammals ate the plant eaters.

The first group of meat-eating mammals was the creodonts. These animals looked and acted much like the meat-eating mammals of today, though they had even sharper teeth. Some creodonts looked like dogs, some looked like ferrets, some looked like hyenas, and so on. The amazing similarities between the creodonts and today's meat eaters suggest that nature has standard patterns, like cookie cutters, out of which new species are made again and again.

The creodonts were eventually replaced by a second group of meat-eating mammals, the carnivores. Carnivores are distinctive for their sharp teeth and powerful jaw muscles for shearing meat. When a carnivore closes its jaws on a piece of meat, its teeth come together like a pair of scissors, cutting the meat in two.

One of the most common carnivores is the dog, which got its start in North America 37 million years ago. The world's first dog was the dawn dog. Small, with a low-slung body and a long tail, the dawn dog looked like a modern fox. Dawn dogs probably traveled in pairs through the forest undergrowth just as foxes do today. Unlike today's foxes, the dawn dog had feet and limbs for climbing and chasing its prey up trees!

CREODONTS, *HYAENODON* AND *TRITEMNODON*.

TREE-CLIMBING DAWN DOGS.

The dawn dog's own family tree branched out to include wolves, coyotes, and others. Six million years ago, dogs crossed the Bering Land Bridge into Asia.

Today wild dogs live on every continent except Antarctica.

PROBOSCIDEANS ▪ Only two elephant species exist today—one in Asia, the other in Africa. The prehistoric world, however, was a veritable circus of about 160 elephantlike species that scientists call proboscideans.

Seventeen million years ago, the first proboscideans migrated to North America from Asia. Called mastodons, these jumbo-sized creatures had long upper tusks and thick coats of reddish-brown hair. They roamed the North American forests in enormous numbers.

Some time after the arrival of the mastodon, another proboscidean made the crossing from Asia. Called *Gomphotherium*, it had a short trunk and two sets of tusks. One set protruded from its lower jaw; the other set protruded from its upper jaw. (An elephant's tusks are incisors that have grown to enormous lengths.)

An even odder-looking proboscidean, *Platybelodon*, weighed four tons and had a 5-foot-long (1.5–meter) lower jaw shaped like a huge shovel. At the end of its jaw were two big flattened incisors.

PLATYBELODON AND GOMPHOTHERIUM (IN BACKGROUND).

Some scientists think that when a "shovel tusker" got hungry, it used its incisors to scrape the bark and strip the leaves off trees. Its upper lip, a modified trunk, pushed the food to the back of its mouth to be chewed by its rear teeth. *Platybelodon* may have kept its front teeth sharp by dragging them along the ground.

MARSUPIALS ▪ For most of its history, North America has not been connected to South America. The Isthmus of Panama, which links the two continents today, didn't exist until 3 million years ago. Once the isthmus was formed, a brisk traffic in species flowed in both directions, which scientists call the Great American Interchange. Those mammals that moved from North to South America included dogs, cats, camels, bears, mastodons, horses, deer, rabbits, and mice. Moving in the opposite direction were armadillos, anteaters, porcupines, opossums, and a group of now-extinct, rhino-sized herbivores known as toxodonts.

The opossum was a unique addition to North America's wildlife. It was the only marsupial to venture north. The majority of the world's marsupials, including kangaroos, koalas, and Tasmanian devils, have lived in South America and Australia. Today, the opossum is still on the move in North America, expanding its territory into the northern United States and Canada.

EDENTATES ▪ Without a doubt, the weirdest immigrants from South America were the glyptodonts. They were members of a group of animals—the edentates—that includes armadillos and anteaters. The biggest glyptodonts were almost as big as compact cars but built like armored trucks. Their bodies were enclosed in a rigid, bony shell, and their heads were capped by a helmet made of the same armor. Some glyptodonts had tails that ended in a large knob bristling with spikes. When threatened, these glyptodonts would swing their tails like medieval knights wielding maces.

Like the high camel and the shovel tusker, the glyptodont was the fulfillment of Cope's Law—that animals tend to get bigger over time. Their appearance in North America heralded the final chapter of the Age of Mammals.

LAND OF THE GIANTS

During the final two million years of the Age of Mammals—the Pleistocene Epoch—North America was a land of giants, or "megafauna."

Imagine yourself scouting a forest close to your Stone Age home 15,000 years ago. Following the shore of a lake, you are struck by the sound of grinding. Turning a corner you see before you, gnawing on a log, a huge beaver!

Six times larger than the beaver we know today, the giant beaver was the size of a black bear. Modern beavers have flat paddle tails that they slap on the

GIANT BEAVER
AND WOOLY MAMMOTHS.

water to warn other beavers of approaching enemies. The giant beaver didn't have a flat paddle tail. Its tail was roundish, like a muskrat's, suggesting that the huge rodent didn't slap its tail on the water. Perhaps a beaver that weighed 400 pounds (180 kilograms) didn't need an alarm signal?

Continuing on your trek, you next encounter a giant ground sloth. Modern sloths spend most of their lives hanging upside-down from the branches of trees in South America. Giant ground sloths grew as tall as trees! The biggest giant ground sloth measured 20 feet (6 meters) from head to tail and weighed three tons. Walking slowly and awkwardly on its knuckles, the great clawed beast could stretch up to browse on the top branches of trees.

Farther along on your trek you spy a herd of woolly mammoths moving in the distance. A close relative of today's elephants, the woolly mammoth had long curved tusks, a peaked head, and a humped, sloping back. Ancient cave paintings made by Stone Age people tell us that the woolly mammoth also had a shaggy coat of hair.

The woolly mammoth was a creature of the Ice Age, which lasted from about 2 million to 12,000 years ago. It lived in large numbers near the great glaciers that covered Canada and the northern United States during that time. Vegetation was scarce on the fringes of the ice sheets. But there was enough of it to support the furry giants, who probably used their tusks to scrape the snow off the grass.

NEVER SMILE AT A SMILODON ▪ Meat-eating animals don't usually reach the size of the biggest plant-eaters. To catch prey, meat-eaters must be fast and agile — two abilities that don't often come with great size.

Still, there were several Pleistocene carnivores that might be called giants. The biggest North American carnivore was the giant short-faced bear. Two to three times more massive than a modern grizzly bear, the giant short-faced bear weighed at least 1,500 pounds (680 kilograms) and could rear up on its hind legs to a height of about 12 feet (4 meters).

The giant short-faced bear's snout gave it a face that looked like a lion's, and its long legs enabled it to run in short bursts as fast as a horse. An awesome enemy, the giant short-faced bear probably preyed on bison, ground sloths, and young mammoths.

Another fierce predator was a saber-toothed cat called *Smilodon*, which means "carving knife tooth." As large as a lion but more massive in build, *Smilodon* was not a fast runner. It relied instead on brute strength and two 6-inch-long (15-centimeter) fangs to bring down its prey.

Smilodon was superbly adapted for death struggles with its victims. Its well-muscled body and large claws gave it the power to hold a victim tight and slash the animal repeatedly with its fangs. Its heavy head coupled with strong neck muscles served to drive the saber teeth through even the toughest hide.

A GIANT GROUND SLOTH
AND A GIANT SHORT-FACED BEAR
SQUARE OFF IN BATTLE.

A GREAT MYSTERY

Twelve thousand years ago, North America was a land of giants—giant beavers, giant ground sloths, giant camels, woolly mammoths, giant short-faced bears, saber-toothed cats. Then they vanished.

The disappearance of the megafauna is one of science's great puzzles. It is natural for a species to exist for a certain length of time and then become extinct. But why did so many big mammals die out at the same time?

One of the most popular extinction theories holds that the giants disappeared due to a rapid change in climate. The last Ice Age ended about 12,000 years ago. As the big glaciers shrank, North America's climate grew warmer and drier very quickly. Many lakes and streams, which served as the animals' watering holes, dried up. Harsh drought led to mass starvation among the big animals, and finally, to their complete extinction.

Some scientists don't agree with that argument, however. They point to evidence showing that the mass extinctions coincided with the widespread settlement of the first North Americans, the Clovis people. Sometime between 14,000 and 12,000 years ago, wandering tribes from Asia crossed the Bering Land Bridge (now covered by water) between Asia and Alaska. From there, the immigrants moved across North America, hunting and gathering as they went.

Some scientists believe that as the Clovis people grew in number, they put enormous pressure on the continent's wildlife. The Clovis people were very successful hunters. In the end, scientists say, they stripped the continent of thirty-one different types of large mammals.

Both extinction theories have their strong points. For now it might be reasonable to say that the giant mammals were under considerable stress in the warmer post-Ice Age climate. The Clovis people delivered the final blows that finished them off.

The extinction of the megafauna is a sad story. Imagine the thrill of seeing those mammalian marvels alive today. Their disappearance should also make us think about our own world. More animals face extinction now than at any other time in modern history. Imagine how much our children and grandchildren would miss today's animals if, like the giant beaver and the woolly mammoth, they too disappeared.

TIMELINE

Years Ago:

65 million	Dinosaurs become extinct. Small mammals begin to flourish.
55 million	The world's first horse, *Hyracotherium*, appears in North America.
45 million	*Uintatherium*, "the most grotesque mammal that ever lived," roams North American forests.
37 million	The world's first dog appears in North America.
3 million	North and South America become connected. Armadillos, porcupines, and opossums enter North America.
2 million	The Ice Age begins, as does the Age of Giant Mammals.
1.5 million	Mammoths migrate to North America from Asia via the Bering Land Bridge.
12,000	The last Ice Age ends. Giant mammals become extinct.

FIND OUT MORE

Age of Mammals by Rupert Matthews (New York: Franklin Watts, 1990).

Mammals by John B. Wexo (Mankato, Minn.: Creative Editions, 1991).

Prehistoric Animals by Daniel Cohen (New York: Doubleday, 1988).

Prehistoric Animals by Peter Zallinger (New York: Random House Books for Young Readers, 1981).

Prehistoric Mammals by Susanne S. Miller (New York: Simon & Schuster, 1984).

INDEX

ABOUT THE AUTHOR

Hugh Westrup is an editor for *Current Science*, a national magazine for children. His articles were chosen for both the 1991 and 1992 editions of *Of Cabbages and Kings: The Year's Best Magazine Writing for Kids*. He is the author of Millbrook Press's *Maurice Strong: Working for Planet Earth* and is a member of The Authors Guild.